FINISHING LINE PRESS
www.finishinglinepress.com

Nonlinear Healing

poems by

Diane Klammer

Finishing Line Press
Georgetown, Kentucky

Nonlinear Healing

ISBN 979-8-89990-539-1 First Edition

Acknowledgments

I would like to thank:

Avocet for publishing Synchronized Swimmers and the Meadowlark
Heavybear for One Hundred Words for Sorrow
Lummox for What a Fisherman said
Open Earth Magazine for Seeing Stars
Wordgathering for Heron's Beak

Heartfelt thanks to Wendy Scher, Lisa Birman and Ann Cooper for editing, Max Regan for organizing suggestions, all at my poetry group for support, Nate Jordon for believing in me, and my family, Aaron, Audrey and Roger for everything they do.

Publisher: Leah Huete de Maines
Editor: Christen Kincaid
Cover and Interior Art: Roger and Diane Klammer
Author Photo: Roger Klammer
Cover Design: Elizabeth Maines McCleavy

Order online: www.finishinglinepress.com
also available on amazon.com

Author inquiries and mail orders:
Finishing Line Press
PO Box 1626
Georgetown, Kentucky 40324
USA

Contents

For my husband of fifty years, Roger, and for our children Aaron & Audrey

Healing is not only a matter of medicine, but of connection to the land, to each other, to the stories that hold us.
Robin Wall Kimmerer

What a Fisherman said at Sawhill Ponds

If you are lucky, white pelicans will land
  forming their fishing circle
    directly in front of you

offer you a singing garland
  of floating gardenias.
    Let nature come to you

See the nests from these trout
  rainbows they make over the pond
    when they jump like that in midair

Muskrats, naturally bashful
  will reveal themselves
    only when you are still

will show you courting rituals
  their nests of woody branch
    their preferred swimming routes

as they glide by you on their backs.
  A painted turtle will swim right next to you
    while the snapping turtle lumbers by in an arc

Townsend's warblers and yellow headed blackbirds
  will show you their gold plumage
    as regal great blue herons

will point the way to gangly legged offspring
  only if you remain peaceful
    while the swallows consume the sunset

Constellations of Cats

(after Majda Gama)

Each cat is wide eyed   awake
woke in a pride of diversity   that will not falter
Fifty-two cats   one for each card in multicolor shuffles   across time
on our ultramarine planet   Sirius watches
a fragile house   our earth   where at home
our president again   withdrew from
the Paris climate agreement
Defiant humpback whales spew fertilizer
which feeds phytoplankton
in upper oceans which capture CO_2
below where red Mars dims   in torrential rain
scientists learn early
not to put stock in wars
for coin   for territorial grabs
Each of us ignites   a brief bioluminescence
in part of a gift cosmos   where living things breathe
Humans falter   Canis Major barks   a myriad of felines prowl
The Cats Eye Nebula shines a reminder of fire and hope

Nonlinear Healing

Days you wake up to ivory enlightened bones
days sharps settle into new threaded wounds

days leap towards crocodile off-key moonhowling
Days gravitate towards snow days pelican times

Humans live in short supply
of what there never is enough of

some days healing feels like peeling
a frozen artichoke to its core

days to avoid each breathing person days
Days to wrap octopus' arms around earth days

People have lost health recoiling from Covid
from our planet's reaction to climate change

days when health care workers pack it in
days doctors smash lunchbox treatment greedily

days hopscotching backwards into chalkboards
Days unidentifiable jay thrills

days peel back layers with naked nail splits
Days healing swells in days crescendo yelps

days in this crowded world of panicked
SUV dwelling bunker survivalists

You might need my help someday
sings a cactus flower lost in the folds of every pillow

days body days spasms constrict lungstrings
Days sonic chambers resonate joysongs

Days to collect confetti pillow feathers to gift
Days to place in left burgundy shirt pockets

Turtle Patience

a jewel box of findings to organize not overwhelm to capture
    to sequence   hold   examine   polish   make sense of
since childhood we gathered   sound bites   of words to   make language
small motor   movements to walk with   then run
yesterday I compiled a song list   called morning   a beginning
a new day is hard to say no to despite news of our country being
disassembled

a painting is a   sum of marks   on canvass becomes an under sea loggerhead
flowers grow some assembled in a vase each one stands out   part of a
bouquet
ingredients in the pot spices   vegetables chicken broth   heat
time makes the stew   turtle patience   it will nourish   delight senses
words on the page   keyboards cursive   design phrases   ideas
can be found everywhere on walls trees book spines   medicine bottles

to scoop up formulate   sound   sense   images   word paintings
anchor them   shape them   arrange them   like notes   on a page
join with like-minded friends   umbrella them in   bend with them
like a legislative body   tell stories among them so they have meaning
beyond any page and us bind them into books   join with others
offer them poems   as collections   beyond the self

To Heal is to Flutter

sand pours from lumbar desert	sandbar	lumbar from desert pours sand
courses in my bloodstream	dream	bloodstream my in courses
a molten symphony of hope	cope	hope of a symphony molten
spine ladder spirals ache rung by rung	spun	rung by rung ache spiral ladder spines
radiant constellations of pain-stained	rain	stained pain of constellations radiant
orange blossom I balance mobility	stilled	mobility balance I blossom orange
lightning endless streams of seventy	levity	seventy streams of endless lightning
one too many races before I knew	unglued	I knew before races one too many
	anew	
my spine was too small for impact	back	impact for my spine was too small
a staircase rail dissolves of	love	of dissolved staircases a rail
inflammation path of chaos	ibis	chaos of path inflammation
flow through neroli milk bee stars	scars	stars bee milk neroli through flow
sting fragrance cosmos orchard	nurtured	orchard cosmos fragrance sting
Venus rotates opposite of earth	worth	earth of opposites rotate Venus
glows electric vodka shots blossom	awesome	blossom shots vodka electric glows
ignites small suns of orange blooms	plumes	blooms orange of suns small ignites
all songs a string every heal a hymn	wind	all hymns heal every string a song

Elegy to California

"Nothing gold can stay"
Robert Frost

If you look closely
    at the Eucalyptus groves in Nipomo California
Los Osos or elsewhere

You may still find a few
    stragglers huddling together
in the fragrant trees

gentle silhouettes
  of the plentiful leaf flames
that once were

#
Tiny ghost fires now burn everywhere
    Monarch Butterflies sputter out
endings of black and orange

insect tales of the past
    portend the future
of extinctions reoccurring

Once millions darkened the sky
      dwindled steadily in the USA
now roughly two thousand remain

Humanity encroaches
    goldrush real estate dwellings
climate change that ever-burning sun flame

Noenicitinoids
    that sickened the honeybees
have collapsed the butterflies too

Civilization erodes California to cinders
    taking flora taking fauna with it
trees emptying in the wake of construction

Good fires bad fires too little water at all
    the sun rises like inflating housing prices
in the golden state

#
earthquake flood
fire and drought
what people have sold
what people have bought

#
Monarchs are only insects
    but someday the mute
will re-inherit California

#
empty houses
vacant condos
empty promises
pandemic legislation

Natural disasters
shaking and smoking
each day away
to nights of blind light

#
fluttering monarchs left
    search for poppy colored milkweed
to feed their unborn

splotches of orange and gold remain
    in a still verdant state
within flame pockets

those who can sleep do
    in a whiny stupor never quite awakening
from long proboscis snores

Synchronized Swimmers

> *"I am like a pelican of the wilderness: I am like an owl of the desert. I watch and am as a sparrow alone upon the house-top."*
> Bible

First there is a sky so laden
with feathery cumulus clouds
that it threatens to burst open.

Then a few descend
into the water like lace paper kites
creating shadows above.

Another glides in
and another until the sky
and lake are inverted

in an orchestra of landing,
a communion of unbroken
grace beneath morning sun.

Twenty-five white pelicans
land on Walden Ponds.
They waterglide in unison,

an ancient gracedance delicate as
snowfall. Slowly these featherboats
pattern into a circle, floating like lotus

flowers, supporting precise instrument bills,
some showing bright orange breeding spots.
White suited synchronized swimmers

tighten the circle, and all at once
dive underwater, tails in air,
to remain for minutes, scooping up

all the fishes they earlier herded
into the lakes center. A few lucky
escaped rainbows thrash whiplike

in shallow water, jumping near the shore.
When finished the pelicans resurface
in synchrony to breathe and rest.

Seeing Stars

For Roger

Is it a negation
of shadow

pin stars
showering a moonless trail

messages
to the milky way

searchlights
in dark matter?

My family and I walk

the Cottonwood Trail July Fourth evening

to escape the crowds

There

and there

fireflies alight
then extinguish

the micro-candles
of their own bodies

My eyesight
is fuzzy

A vitreous detachment

provokes brilliant flashes of light
at the upper periphery

interrupts vision
with rapid dot-dashes
of nerve

Together we watch

Miniature volcanoes blink
"I'm here"

and "Fooled you"
defy space
tease

open doors
shut them
showing off

tiny hearths
elfin campfires

fairy dust
in boggy fields.

Fireworks
from Folsom stadium
and beyond
illuminate our senses

scribble the sky
with paint scrawls

reflect questions
to dim the stars

I faintly see
fire flowers
watered by
the Big Dipper comets meteors

I stand   I imagine
sparklers
Ferris wheels strung with white lights

Bits of   electric   visual
Morse code

blinding composition
of neurons behind membranes
paint my eyes

arrows of streaking   luminescence
that turn   gold
and will soon
strobe off

My son holds   a flashlight

on the edge
of dimming out

Streetlights above us
suddenly go dark
as ghosts might
hover behind trees in the wind
tricking me once more
to see retinal flashes of light

behind my eyelashes
My family's chatter becomes
bells

to chime us home
amidst fading images
as the show ends
A storm approaches
Thunder claps
Lightning

pierces the sky

letting the rain spill out
onto July fourth
like any day

Heron's Beak

Maybe it's birdsong, as
to own a bird, one must live
in a house of glass walls.

Once sciatica became mine,
it became mine forever.
Birdsong can be piercing,

especially in night's awakening.
Birdsong can be soothing.
What is that warbler's message?

Call it a neural communication,
a sharp throb to tell me
to stop doing whatever

I am doing. A lengthy story
of what will happen if
I persist with the same

motion, firing axons
and dendrites warning
me not to keep going.

Call it mitochondrial zap,
a kick in the spine
with steel-toed shoes.

Call it the red- yellow-
green light of throb,
the on again off again.

Call it gratitude
when it fizzles out—
dissipates—gives way—

a space to stretch out again
like a heron in flight, a
Great Blue with a piercing

beak which can put out an eye,
but when the heron flies from
its nest to land on a pond,

call it interlude between pain,
a flight from tree nest to lake
Call it relief—the water-dance,

that swim to relieve the burning—
When the herons are joined by
a flock of white pelicans,

we are all synchronized
swimmers in water the pool.
When I swim, I am soaring as

a heron flies on the air's currents,
looks down into aqua blue depths,
looks up to sky as feather clouds

change shape before my eyes.
Call it lightning and thunder,
before the burning returns,

when we all must get out
to shore for safety reasons.
Call it weight of the world,

when I climb out on ladder—
step by step—to be
earthbound, gravity bound again

like a heron again walking on
land looking gangly and awkward.
Agony immediately descends.

It is a long distance back,
not a mere squint through
binoculars as far becomes near.

Call it success—to make it
through another moment. Call it
jellyfish sting. Call it fire ant bite.

Call it pillow down when sleep
robs the hurt—erases the pain
and I magic carpet my dreams.

Next Time Around

I have searched everywhere to find it anywhere
from an out of body swoop awake on downy back
plumage of a Great Blue Heron flying sideways
for torn answers scrawled incomplete on sand grains

abandoned shells stuffed in bottles crushed
in stuck moss ready to root from soil in flux
to crust underneath every library book written
in weeds with earth detritus hung Nitrobacter

spoken in a low voice of pleas stifled questions
of whispered authority at a castles moat bottom
propelled backwards from lifecycles Mourning
Cloak butterfly cocoon caterpillar egg mosaic

leaves from tatters of climate devastation stories
we have not yet experienced in planet full force
to find one tear-soaked remnant poem to explain
An antidote recipe for human destruction of earth

More Variants of Covid with Wasp Stings

A poppy not crimson
not burnt orange
not meadowlark yellow

a combination of these
with a gas blue base
ignites the bones

not sap green
ivory white serpentine
a fire in the spine burns

water eases the pain
does not douse the flame
renders it less stabbing

until gravity puts it down
back into the flames again
prairie fields igniting

under more summer rain
of horizontal sleep
until morning sun blazes

awake to fiery blood
morning coffee clouds
flame under teakettle

a fuzzy grey look
of haze or nature
gnarly blue spruce

rain just beginning to fall
a submarine joy blind
as perusal of confinement

Covid enter with stealth
spreads itself
in intricate announcement

a fever migraine
of inflammation
from sore cough throat

with body aches
elfin campfires toasting marshmallows
into bees followed by fireflies

devoid of taste or smell
a viral biochemistry
comprehension of human genome sequence

vampire of daylight
nerve changing vision
as pines remain silent

Mariposas Monarca

there they soared in the state of Michoacan
tiny marigold mariposas in midair so many
they eclipsed the sunshine with brilliant wings
sky painted waves of blood orange so thickly

trees painted fire coins of gold wanderers
fluttering over small patches of ultramarine
sky each a pequena flor de la vida la Muerte
tiny flowers innocent of all deaths beneath them

in a sanctuary so peligroso their guardians killed
in 2020 seis en total murieron in a place of safety
what can these shiny copper penny fliers do when
tiny lives of their protectors become snuffed out

today they remain endangered as habitat becomes
scarcer from Mexico to Canada where some make
annual migrations so amazing for fourth generation
all North America must work as one to keep them

Chemical companies drug cartels of money murders
assesinatoes de hombres de dinero climate warming
neonics habitat deterioration powers that be create
un mundo feo desprovisto de polinzadores de la vida

Caesura

a one note song
after a few false starts
Maestra raises her hand

a pregnant pause
one drumbeat in time
where paramecium divide

a space in between
snowdrop arcs
a place of hesitation

frozen rock collapses
into our steam fumarole
few take responsibility for

a snowflake is born
one single moment unfurls
our earth's next ice age

Overwintering Diminishment

A method of copper dresses in
wish breathe leaves float in manage
scary rose gold cymbal ecstasy
under mango shakes Idaho to apple
core lemon striped licorice popsicle
melts under midnight orange flags
Ills sont tellerment fatigues maintenant.

a method of copper quiet flame
sings infinity scales foxtails wag
paint Monarchs drip amber honey
dragons crawl from scales
rise to treetop repetition leaf
twist in striped yellow gown
emerge dripping wet flecks

a method of copper volcanoes
deep Jello of cornflakes harps
wing edged life mixes in gilt
silence spun out from yellow
silks press filament flags flap
from marigold mariposa spirits
from sunrise skies combustion

a method of copper wood boxes
green trees spring into paper lit
books sit fecund with allergy spores
heavy clouds silver threaded presents
bisects days of sun in swallowtail
amazement walks through rose garden
La Terre est-elle devenue malade?

a method of copper zinnias deep red
stacks of wood matches hatch burn
the wanderer dragon alights on
new trunks eggs stolen do not appear
easily pine tree half grub retreat
auburn paintbrush fills overwintering
groves to new nectar wining grape

Collaborative Earth Poem

Wake up! Outside the earth is spinning. Call, respond.
One long-lashed eye turns in profile. The world cushion:
a blue wool hat with brown marled fur, a blue streak
locked on each gesture, on stillness, silhouetted velvet
against bright bars, monologues and diatribes, imagine:
each of us is a torn fragment avoiding the phone, activity,
running, eclipsed by a pair of glitter scissors, hair askew.
I say: The world is a tsunami, struggling to find clues.
My head sings, its leaves of maple sing matchsticks,
the earthy duff of early autumn, Celtic harp music.
I could love those sounds: a jay splashes, then a song,
Bach or Brahms, the ephemeral rise and dark falling
from squabbling siblings, a cricket's chirp, the doe, owls,
the music, the lilt, patterns. It rocks our soul's high solo.
A mother's caress. Just imagine this is the very last time
you will ever hear her voice. Eyes on herself, spinning.
Now I am searching for answers. Does it get easier? Listen.
We Need Each Other. Need burns like a torch.

(from the work & words of Trisha Zembruski, Diane Klammer,
Wendy Scher & Cass Tunick)

Koi Mandala

haiku

cobalt lakes renew
apple blossoms mix sunlight
burst flame in going

moon over koi ponds
secrets whisper in fin strokes
swimmers dream in schools

strength born in summer
Koi welcome rapid cloudscapes
under tornadoes

shimmers in darkness
jump splash out in triumph
laughter of koi fish

crimson scales ignite
fierce elements of copper
butterfly arcades

leaves drift in old gold
koi gobble grass at harvest
corn husks fill the pond

snowdrifts veil the ice
warm beneath koi fold fin wings
dragons wait to rise

from thawed streams return
leap in cascades overflow
koi circles candle paths

Meditations on Avian Flight

"To comprehend a crow, you must have a crow's mind."
Arthur Sze

Uplift from air currents can overcome sadness

How does flight happen?

Seagulls and ravens **ride air currents**
answer the call to launch themselves from an ocean cliff

and be caught by the air's uplift

That sailplane sensation **free fall** almost straight down to the rocks
then at the last second a one eighty degree turn upwards

How does a bird defy gravity and fly upwards?

From dips and dances to **rise like feathers** do
Energy lightness of body wing shape with airlift to bone **light**
curves to sky

What is the avian view from the air?

A vast **expanse of** sand foam candle wave fizzles
from cerulean blue ocean to shoreline

great heart cockles angels' wings sand dollars scallops
onlookers on blankets umbrellas children build sand castles

and leave pink rose petals on the beach
to **spell migration**

jellyfish dolphins nurse sharks whales swim flying fishes glide egrets fly

Do birds have charts for brains   Maps in their head?

A Birds navigational apparatus allows them **compel**s
them to fly south for winter   directs them how

In flocks   alone   in V shaped patterns   over water around planes
barriers
some become pelagic and feast   off rock islands in an ocean's middle

What do birds think about when they fly?

Pelicans scrawl **full loops** descend to Heron Pond at Pella Crossing
for fun quibbling   or out of necessity   to land to feed

A few seem to **ascend to the sun** in their line of vision as Icarus **find**
food each other nesting **find** resting nooks on the cliffs in open water

soar closer to their destination with **wingbeat** after **wingbeat**

until the birds **recognize**

Can a bird remember? Can a bird reason?   **yes**

They **sojourn** where they need to be

To comprehend a crow, you must have a crow's mind

Uplift from air currents can overcome sadness

How does flight happen?

Seagulls and ravens **ride air currents**
answer the call to launch themselves from an ocean cliff

and be caught by the air's uplift

That sailplane sensation **free fall** almost straight down to the rocks
then at the last second a one eighty degree turn upwards

How does a bird defy gravity and fly upwards?

From dips and dances to **rise like feathers** do
Energy lightness of body wing shape with airlift to bone **light**
curves to sky

What is the avian view from the air?

A vast **expanse of** sand foam candle wave fizzles
from cerulean blue ocean to shoreline

great heart cockles angels' wings sand dollars scallops
onlookers on blankets umbrellas children build sand castles

and leave pink rose petals on the beach
to **spell migration**

jellyfish dolphins nurse sharks whales swim flying fishes glide egrets fly

Do birds have charts for brains   Maps in their head?

A Birds navigational apparatus allows them **compel**s
them to fly south for winter   directs them how

In flocks   alone   in V shaped patterns   over water around planes
barriers
some become pelagic and feast   off rock islands in an ocean's middle

What do birds think about when they fly?

Pelicans scrawl **full loops** descend to Heron Pond at Pella Crossing
for fun quibbling   or out of necessity   to land to feed

A few seem to **ascend to the sun** in their line of vision as Icarus **find**
food each other nesting **find** resting nooks on the cliffs in open water

soar closer to their destination with **wingbeat** after **wingbeat**

until the birds **recognize**

Can a bird remember? Can a bird reason?   **yes**

They **sojourn** where they need to be

R&D

Mating Flight

"Awaiting the gold blade of their hurry"
Jorie Graham

They floated skyward
|singularly & cloudlike|
hundreds of tiny
foreign winged creatures
in my own back yard
when I was nine or so
in Sun Valley California
They poured out of a small cavern
in their ant hill of discarded pebbles
seed bead gems on sand
winged red ruby &
black onyx exclamations
scurrying |heedless
of me and the mockingbirds
horned lizard ~ wind|
Then all at once |one by one| soared
compelled by primal will |pheromones|
in swarms dotting the sun
Firedrakes| dragons riding
air currents above as I| blinded
by sunlight| looked away
marveling at their flight
How could red ants| subterranean
for most of their life
|without pilot's lessons|
just take to the skies and fly
In air princes and princesses
mate repeatedly
in a stunning arial orgy
Much later |exhausted|
~survivors land |separately
disoriented helpless zigzagging
on hard ground rocks blades of grass
|lost without assistance|
I did not know then| that for drones
it was a fated double death

petite mort ecstasy followed
by actual mortality from helpless
starvation or predation
I learned that the sole
purpose of the drone was to mate
and then perish
|That day~ I lost some of my fear
of surrendering my virginity|
Cruel single-minded nature
Surviving mated queens
bite off their wings
start new colonies
|a giant task|
Roles morph slightly with age| but
are designated shortly after birth|
Drones have no say in what they do
after becoming themselves
They are pampered fed cleaned
until the big day |nuptial flight holds
a surreal utilitarian
mechanized beauty| determined
fueled with seemingly little to no
self-awareness |a stark
compulsive cold reality|
Do drone ever wonder in
their lives about love
purpose happiness or legacy
|Or do they just sail to
the nuptial flight|
& hold to them that one
moment of triumph

For the Children

After Fady Joudah

When in college biology
I captured a fire queen ant
and put her in an aquarium
where she settled down
began to lay eggs underground

After five days despite food
water from cotton wool
she seemed to catch my scent
became anxious found the surface
started pacing the perimeter

I let them go in the backyard
In less than a week
she realized she was captive
and knew her offspring
would not be safe as refugees

One Hundred Words for Sorrow

Thousands of dolphins are slaughtered in Taiji.
How can sunrise be peppered with such death?
Too much wailing happens before midday.
Before the murdering, a mother cradles her young.

Children do not understand levels of mercury rising.
Waves leave blood prints on stones at morning.
Can any ray of light reach this kind of suffering?
A harvest moon brightens when she honors a newborn.

Dolphins recognize their reflections in a mirror.
White birds flee from darkness where innocents die.
Blossoms fall from bridges into a helpless ocean.
These lines contain one hundred words for sorrow.

Where did you First Fall?

When was the first time you understood our planet as separate wonder?
Not on streets of concrete, telephone wire lines of automobiles, but count
endangered scales of Monarch butterflies' golden egrets and heron plumes
of white pelicans feathering entire lake swallowtail tremble earthquake to
stop ants in tracks play with mudpies dig earthworm sandcastles heart cockles
clay land loam grass squishes in toes sand crabs to tickle fingers Can you
study a stamp with a peregrine falcon on it. So many starlings encircle sun,
fireflies warm, sea holds you up lover waves, you surf to shore sand in suit
Did your desert ear pursue horned lizard heart pulses beneath thumb and
forefingers? Where did you smell tuberose, plant a garden, crunch a zucchini?
When did you travel from city to mountains, raft a river hide in a cavern?
Make love underneath Half Dome in a tent by your own campsite cedar fire.
Behold desert sunrise sit shotgun to Kings Canyon with father driving,
savoring incense from a forest fire, mountain lion prints under bluebelly lizard
pushups. How long flat on back to make shapes in clouds, study constellations
dizzying spin hum of gentle Italian bees in pepper tree above head crack
walnuts on ground? Have you tasted fresh trout, faced false charge from black
bear in back country? Where did you spend days in fire tower lighthouse
contemplating your unfolding? Where did you fall in love with inhabitants of
earth whom you do not resemble? Explain your legacy to climate change &
what you would put in time capsule?

Floating Lanterns

"Wait on the wind, catch a scent of salt, call it our life."
Philip Levine

Now the jellyfish float by the ferry
like golden steppingstones

inviting us to climb underneath
a red moon while stepping on their backs.

When Christ walked on water,
He probably paused on a humid

evening to walk on floating lanterns,
pumpkin gelatin fire umbrellas

while chartreuse phosphorescence
embroidered His white robes.

Each drop of seawater holds
all secrets of the universe,

from the atoms to the protists
to the molecules in the bodies

of giant humpback whales,
chorusing song for the conch.

All these droplets move through jellyfish,
undulating corpuscles, rainbow Medusae.

We cannot touch them with our feet,
fallen and stung species that we are.

Where were you the day our food supply collapsed?

"The keeping of bees is like the direction of sunbeams."
Henry David Thorough

A honeybee's buzz takes 11,400 wing strokes per minute to make.
It takes 500 bees to make a pound of honey.
A colony of bees has over 40,000 honeybees and one queen. ez
Bees visit 2 million flowers and fly fifty-five miles to make a pound of honey.

Is it fall already,
dying brood?

For what purpose came this intricate happenstance?

Picture with your compound brains, az

an amber spill
floating in rivers.

An unwanted vision, this

Would Blake call death of the hexagon "fearful symmetry?"

Frank L. Baum was high on hash at the time. oz
Pass the pipe to Oppenheimer, Mr. Monsanto.

Low diving stinger,
to a bear, a bee is a god. uuuuuuz

Intricate chaos dribbles in the hollow of this tree.

Long Covid with Bee Stings

1
Thick as orange amber   or liquid honey
ontogeny
        head to toe neuron bodies

recapitulates   tells a story old as
        memory muscle scramble   recovery unfurls in flower vines

phylogeny   an evolutionary sequence needed for vaccine development
        A Genomic Code
covid vaccines   give rise to   idiopathic hearing loss

ears buzz louder than a distant locomotive arriving like a myriad of cicadas
        to crossroads cars mirroring lives

Dissonance in auditory   resonance such as bells ring
        host cumulus elevates to insect fields under sun

Crickets sing summer songs hum with Italian bees
        frog choruses announce summer's endone last day in August

        of windy Indian summer farewells
        September rounds melted corners
gives generous rise to autumn ash rainbows

muscles hum and eyes burn while wild bees fly over zinnia fields
        Bell's palsy rings out
nerves still slack around the right nostril regenerate
        nerves sizzle and twitch to lift   pumpkins are harvested

pain echoes translate to inflammation   like wasp stings
        makes movement difficult   manifests to heal
axon & dendrites mis fire   a grasshopper quivers and jumps
        hummingbird moth   hits net   struggles to escape

lifegiving oxygen rises through   a garden in late summer
        Recovery is calendar slow
coleoptera on sunflower   an ant clings to cornflowers
        lazy bumblebees hover and soar as lightening

nerves refire   a meadowlark sings goodbye symphonies to mental fuzziness

with clear long notes

Long Covid Vaccines

2
[redacted]
[redacted] bodies

[redacted] tells a story old as
memory [redacted] [redacted] recovery [redacted]ls [redacted]

[redacted] [redacted] [redacted] needed [redacted] vaccine development
A Genomic Code
covid vaccines [redacted] [redacted]

[redacted]
[redacted] lives

[redacted] resonance such as bells ring
[redacted]

[redacted]
[redacted] one last day in August

[redacted]

muscles hum and eyes burn [redacted] [redacted] [redacted] fly over zinnia fields
[redacted] palsy rings out
nerves still slack around the right nostril [redacted]
nerves sizzle and twitch to lift [redacted]

pain echoes translate to inflammation like wasp stings
makes movement difficult manifests to heal
axon & dendrites mis fire [redacted]
[redacted] [redacted] escape

lifegiving oxygen rises through [redacted]
[redacted]
coleoptera on sunflower [redacted]
[redacted]

nerves refire [redacted]

with clear long notes

Long Covid Recovery

3
Thick as orange amber   or liquid honey
ontogeny
head to toe neuron bodies

recapitulates   tells a story old as
memory muscle scramble   recovery unfurls in flower
vines

phylogeny   an evolutionary sequence needed for vaccine development
a genomic code
covid vaccines   give rise to   idiopathic hearing loss

ears buzz louder than a distant locomotive arriving like a myriad of
cicadas
to crossroads cars mirroring lives

Dissonance in auditory   resonance such as bells ring
host cumulus elevates to insect fields under sun

Crickets sing summer songs   hum with Italian bees
frog choruses announce summers end one last day in August

of windy Indian summer farewells
September rounds melted corners
gives generous rise to autumn ash rainbows

muscles hum and eyes burn while wild bees fly over zinnia fields
Bell's palsy rings out
nerves still slack around the right nostril regenerate
nerves sizzle and twitch to lift   pumpkins are harvested

pain echoes translate to inflammation   like wasp stings
makes movement difficult   manifests to heal
axon & dendrites mis fire   a grasshopper quivers and jumps
hummingbird moth   hits net   struggles to escape

lifegiving oxygen rises through   a garden in late summer
Recovery is calendar slow

coleoptera on sunflower an ant clings to cornflowers
lazy bumblebees hover and soar as lightening

nerves refire a meadowlark sings goodbye symphonies to mental fuzziness

Post Fusion Flareup

Not a swine or a serpent or red ant or remnants of swoon	moon
but a woman born with a congenitally small spine older	shoulder
Locust tree leaves fall yellow ellipses reminiscent	luminescent
of amber honeybees caught in updrafts of ember	September
warm early autumn late summer wind gusts each one	gone
a syllable of spiral blazes in her spine fine line fire	pyre
memory pollen from that orange tree from childhood	neighborhood
where poetry of discoveries grew when she was flexible	indelible
neroli inflammation grows now at seventy-one blooms	brooms
out of season weaves perfume garlands electric excruciates	weights
from right hip back psoas muscles to legs whole body	oddity
clicks code from ceiling fan to venom bee stings	brings
metronome screams from sting of scorpion ant or	lore
aphid just a cry of hungry blue jay outside for peanuts	freedom
spiral staircase of mobility collapses just a sidewind	windchime
viper shedding skin harmless rosy boa within her	skin
reticulated serpentine back fusion gone wrong	belong
in marrow throat of misfiring nerve endings	bending
Firecrackers pop inside muscle spasms cannot	fraught
move agony of going nowhere still hurts prone	alone
glass shards of beak egrets cuts clean spun fiber	stirs
clouds knot her down inside gravity corridors	scores
she becomes a crooked guitar that plays only minor	liner
chords not laughter of childhood limber cartwheels	feels
but agonized wails knife bow of taut string breaks	mistakes
childhood Valencia orange tree blossoms hypnotic	melodic

her body holds thousands of buzzsaws jingling   singing
honeybees' flower heavy pulls towards center   enter

earth core over septic tanks of sodden roots lose ground   around
from mockingbird divebomb feathers chemical reactions   captions

of her mind pages turn in dreams of old houses ablaze float   compote
pyres of inflamed nerves escape fractured axon to dendrite   bite

light of ignites only escape is disturbed sleep from Prednisone   alone
glass rivers of molten misfiring her spine a bent question of why   lullabies

keeps her awake for a pain pill she will not take it hurts simply to   do
breathe from hollows of her lung's circulation forest of poet trees   deity

brachial pulse with sparks of a single sun a teacup chip throbbed   sobbed
of bloodstream water allows brief respite season of sleep blank tide   cried

carries her to horizons beyond her spine swims through galaxies   alleys
of milky stars oceans waves break out of breath tides change curl   unfurl

Beyond darkness blank horizons resolve MRI images stem cell   tour
injections spine home through libraries cathedrals of organs drone   zone

capsules of sweat of heal slowly propels self where she must go   flow
prisms of a single molecule her body wound breaks free   breathe

At Opening

It took five years for them to find that house
made for bluebirds chickadees said the builder
Western bluebirds grow bigger round hole yawns
large will it let predators find them hosts worry

avian chickadee refugees welcome within
a pair of black capped perpetual motion flight
wanderers took over the front yard we cannot
step outside without a stern chickadee scolding

we voyeurs can peer through blinds but not peer in
our guesswork curves around every corner enclosed
within that birdhouse humbly offered we must not
see the inner workings tiny heads hover at opening

if only we had birdhouse with camera for our wonders
spy work to see the action inside as birds guard door
imagine raising a family while predators lurk nearby
not a moments peace in songbird household making

discovery nest building egg laying young feeding we
observe brood moves with online chickadee webcam
stalking while we sound mental alarm when gardeners
squirrels racoons jays cats people lurk by too closely

I Call to you like Crickets

1.
My song to you fills up the strange universe
hidden by Ponderosa pine needles
My love's resonance is like the crisp air after the last string has just stopped humming

2.
Morse code of star shine and new song

3.
I am a straddling child of two cultures simple tongued
I hope this song will not get lost within the rest of the noises calling through the mountains

4.
We are all part of one song like rain showers
on elephant ear leaves

5.
All my life my seemingly voiceless heart was ever calling to you in the multitudes of names calling
A prayer rings out to you to return unspoken again then spoken
in sonic light that guides me in my long journey to find you

Fireflies in Summer

(split double ghazal) after Clif Mason

He is a kind eyed man
whose love burns
too intensely to sustain in summer
from his hands he offers fireflies

the way he embraces me
in a nighttime breeze of fireflies
I owe so much
to the brief summer

my eyes gaze at him all night long
in haze before morning
pink dawn is nothing at all
to the realm of fireflies

memories hold imagination
fodder for dreams
their music haunts me
in rhythm of a dance in summer

calendar days of life
obscure the reality of him
in flower fields of sunlight
that mutes starshine of fireflies

I will not turn
my gaze from his face
his eyes mirror back to mine
in cool evenings of summer

those songs we sing
play drumbeats electric
morse code in my heart
on and off flashes of fireflies

the embers I hold
burn my cupped hands
I cannot keep that glow
alive forever in summer

vestiges of lives burn to die
in imperfect mortality
as I well know
the nature of fireflies

before the distant rains
comes a muted sizzle of flames
to illuminate what love sustains
to soothe in heat of a long summer

A Quartet of Feather Blues

I merely took the energy it takes to pout and wrote some blues.
Duke Ellington

I
Great Blue Herons

A prehistoric ballerina
covered in blue feathers

flew over a gray pond
at Pella Crossing

blending with silver water
mirroring a cottonwood grove

Everything about her
gangly on land

graceful in air
Another twilight flier

landed on water
danced open winged

shimmering as if they in tandem
had practiced for thousands

of centuries with the shamans
Twenty-first century

pterodactyls live together
in condominiums with an

aerial view of the ponds
mothers hovering over babies

with gangly legs hanging underneath
It's coming and going

of dancing dragons
that impresses the most

when they fly into a fire
sunset to look like gods

stepping only on water
before disappearing

reed like into the shoreline
at twilight before

spearing that last fish
to bring back to the rookery

II
Turning to the Blues

I play BB Kings Blues
on the stereo
one weekend morning

I turn to music to lift
my spirits while preparing
my home for guests

Research has proven
shades of blue
elevate the mood

So does singing
the blues. They fly out
with the voice and vanish

The Jays call for peanuts.
There is traffic on the feeder
singing in the yard

Suddenly a Lazuli Bunting
visits outside
My mood soars

III
To Own a Bird

Blue Jay taps on her sliding patio door
with pointed black beak
beneath an indigo crest

A black necklace
adorns intelligent eyes
above a velvet feather belly

The bird flaps brilliant blue wings
fanning them rapidly at his side
begging like a child dancing

in an out-sized denim shirt
knocking down boundaries
with feathers and charm

She holds out peanuts
in the shell which he takes
from her open hand

Today the Stellar's Jays are restless
Flickers, goldfinches, and doves
swoop down, rapidly feeding

They hear the wind in the pines
sense a thunderstorm brewing
above locust trees

To own a bird, she must live
content in a house of glass and light
fully visible to those free flying by

IV
Superficial Sameness

Fast fliting feather mess of gorgeous coloration
Blue jays call my backyard home each morning

this is where the similarity ends in a peanut pile
that transforms each bird into a parody of itself

a hungry peanut picker and tapper scarfs it down a
broken shelled nut immediately after picking it up

then an indecisive compulsive hopper weighs each shell
several times before ending up with first one it touched

a timid approach avoidance nut pile stalker is chased off
by another more aggressive jay before it can get a nibble

an aggressive one spends more time chasing off other jays
and squirrels than trying to eat and leaves after a display

of arial midair clashes of feathers and squawks which luckily
rarely occur but build up into a frenzy that empties the yard

as all fly to nearby trees to clear heads while constant screecher sits
on a blue spruce limb yelling nonstop like a fledgling probably full

above in air is the dive bomber that purposefully barely misses my
head scarily as it swoops and makes me think of bats instead of jays

behold the painfully slow creeper that pecks one from my hand to
fly off quickly to a distant cottonwood in an arc like it never met me

there is the pooper and the flapper and the distant birdbath drinker
the robber of bird feeders the showoff feather shaker post preener

My family and I love them all

The Meadowlark

The man whispered, "God, speak to me." And a meadowlark sang.
Unknown

You don't have to be on the Grand Tour
underneath the Sistine Chapel,

on a beach in Provence, out in Kings canyon,
or anywhere except in the realm of your imagination.

Yet every second counts, ticks the clock,
sings the meadowlark, says the beating of your heart

with the virtuosity of Paganini,
simply by knowing what it knows.

There is no reason to go anywhere at all.
But if you do, notice every detail.

The way Michelangelo created his paintings
to reach out larger than life only to you.

The way the waves on the beach bow
before sacrificing their bodies on the shore.

The way Abert's Squirrel slides through
the Ponderosa Pine as it parts just for her.

The way the Black Capped Chickadee sings
as it flies downward on a slant.

The way the sun feels on your face through Ponderosas
as you smell the vanilla running sap.

You can tell your story to the whole world
and it will tell you, its story.

The only thing you must do is listen,
before joining in song with all the spinning earth.

Humming

> *"A day without beauty and*
> *pain is not complete.*
> *Aren't they two wings*
> *of the same bird?"*
> *Len Anderson*

1
Our bodies mimic perfection
of hive and honeybee, both
designed with efficient symmetry.
And like the sting of the honeybee
our minds ignite
for clearer understanding
of the watermark of our own existence.

Our cells burn with each individual story
from mitochondrial DNA.
Millions of years have evolved,
returning to millions of stars.
Humans have envisioned the heavens
to explain the mysteries
beyond the grave
throughout history.

Bound to earth,
we hold partial knowledge
of gravity
of the earth's core.

Wingless we want to ascend
in an imagined afterlife
rising with the deities we create,
discarding the confinement of
our slouching worn bodies, easing
away from pain and uncertainty

There is wisdom in trying to answer impossible questions
ever foolish, ever hungry, ever guessing.

2

My back throbs
as I wander through a field
of zinnias underneath the sun,
flowers of every color alive
with humming and buzzing of insects,
honeybees, bumblebees, grasshoppers
going about collective business of making a living.

I used to run so I felt as if I were flying.
Today, my body feels as if every
cell has been stung,
burning up. Still
I thirst for knowledge,
long for beauty,
collect flowers in a basket as I rest
on a cane, think beyond me
to the flying creatures, the fairies
dragons, angels.

I read about facts of science
on the tiny internet in my hand.
Yet I feel baffled even in a field with scores
of bees buzzing above me, jays screeching for food,
an aviary in the locust tree.

Nothing is perfect,
not even the most sophisticated
mathematical equations
which explain the flight of bird and bumblebee,
the mysteries of the architecture
of the hive.

I must accept the lack of knowledge
of the structure of the vertebrae
inside me, how to heal it,
the fact that mine has not responded to
fusion, laminectomy, treatments to relieve

its pain

3

Our creator is to be forgiven for
only allowing us to solve
some of the questions in life
in any given moment.
We know that doctors
like the rest of us only have written
an incomplete score.
Science has come so far
from bloodletting and leeches
to knowledge of biochemical interactions,
painkillers, surgical procedures that succeed, that fail.

We must all go on with our own singing,
our own notation even if each note hurts.
our incomplete existence holds complete meaning,
A paradox not unlike this beauty and this pain.

It was only yesterday
that the flight of bumblebees
could be explained by the laws of physics,
Today we don't completely comprehend
why our honeybees fall,

but none of us are afforded the luxury of giving up
trying to comprehend our planet, ourselves.
We all contribute to the humming of the cosmos.

My body may be humming with pain
but it is still humming.
Like every large and infinitesimal creature,
I sing with the one voice I've been given.

Gratitude

"When the owl sings, the night is silent."
Charles de Leusse

As
I
Run
In
An
Open
Field
A
Silent
Shadow
Covers
Me
as I am grateful not to be a mouse.
A
Great
Horned
Owl
Flies
Overhead
Erasing
Me
With
His
Giant
Wingspan

Diane Klammer was born in Sun Valley, California and lives in Boulder, Colorado with her husband, Roger. She is a writer, poet, musician, painter, therapist and retired biology teacher. She and her husband painted the cover for her third book, *Nonlinear Healing* and images within. This book explores the interconnectedness of nature and healing in a time when it is especially important to notice and derive strength from the beauty of the earth while we still can.

Her grown children live in Santa Clara and Alameda, California. Her writing interests include nature, sports, psychology and healing. Her work had appeared in *Rattle, Lummox, Pudding, Avocet, Spaces, Wordgathering, Syncopation Review,* forthcoming in the *Missing Slate* and others, and in Canada, Australia, Wales, England, Scotland and Ireland., She is bicultural, her mother from Bahia, Brazil and father, Scandinavian American.

She keeps a blog on WordPress, *Dianeklammerpoetry* where you can see images of paintings, photography, songs, stories, essays and poems. *Love, Love* is her second book (2021) after *Shooting the Moon* (2009). She tries to approach her work with a spirit of compassion, humor and honesty. She is grateful for all writers who continue the ongoing conversation of poetry in all its forms.

www.ingramcontent.com/pod-product-compliance
Lightning Source LLC
LaVergne TN
LVHW091132110726
842587LV00004B/157
9798899905391